Praise for *Courage: Living from the Heart, Heroes Revealed*

In this singular collection, poet Pamela Warren Williams keeps counsel with a wise raven—not Poe's, but Rebecca Brewer's—to connect readers to the less-told stories of diverse human heroes, like the curandera of Silver City, forevermore. Like those she honors—from the taxi driver who, mid-fare, abandons his vehicle to save people from a burning building, to a young, outspoken survivor of a school shooting, Warren Williams responds to what this moment in history demands: unadorned truth, humility, and action. Reading the stories before the poems enhances one's appreciation for the spark of spirit, courage, and sacrifice that first captured the poet's imagination. The book is an invitation to learn more about the lives and work of her forty-two subjects, and to embrace our own heroism by stepping up, in word and deed, to do good and do it well.

—Andi Penner, PhD, Author, *Upcycled: Poetry Repurposed* (2024)

Such a powerful honoring of how interconnected our lives are, how the stories of others weave intimately with our own. I'd wager none of these heroes would imagine they'd one day be the subject of a poem, much less honored in a book called Courage. This collection is an inspiration to be a more honest, more loving, more generous, more courageous human.

—Rosemerry Wahtola Trommer,
Author, *The Unfolding* and host of The Poetic Path

When life serves up adversity, conflict, strife, it is natural to lose hope, to get broken down by negativity and a growing sense of futility. In *Courage: Living from the Heart*, Pamela Warren Williams offers us the opportunity to be inspired by real-life heroes, otherwise ordinary folks who under extraordinary circumstances chose to act in selfless, altruistic, community-building ways.

Each hero shares the qualities of putting concerns for their own safety and wellbeing secondary to saving others, righting a wrong, making the world a better place, of truly living their values. I found myself reading the poem, then the bio, then the poem again. The writing is sublime and instead of drawing attention to itself through craft or artifice, Warren Williams allows the focus to be on the acts of, and sometimes cost of, heroism. Some examples:

Athlete Peter Norman, ostracized and penalized for his act of altruism.

Rebecca Brewer: "Stories of her journey / laden with holes and mysteries. / The known astounding in its breadth."

Kevin McKay, "who appeared suddenly as a hero. Sometimes, one simply rises to the demands of the moment."

Shavarsh Karapetyan diving into a cold, murky lake water: "Thirty-Five feet down, / the finswimming champion kicked out / a window of the wrecked streetcar, / pulling thirty-seven to safety / one at a time."

Haydée Santamaría, whose "unique role within the Casa de las Americas allowed her to practice internationalism . . . creating a safe container for artists and intellectuals from around the world to meet and collaborate and giving a voice to countless bold women around the globe."

Kaze Gadway, responding to the "fallout of our crumbling economy / and fractured healthcare system."

Warren Williams reminds us what a hero is. Gods are born with super-human powers and strength; a hero is a mere mortal who achieves an elevated status through courage, ingenuity, conviction, altruistic decisions and above all, action.

—JOSEPHINE LORE WWW.JOSEPHINELOREPOET.COM

Some people are biologically and psychologically "wired" to help others due to enhanced neural sensitivity, such as a more active or larger amygdala that better recognizes fear and distress in others. This altruistic drive is often supported by a "helper's high," where helping releases endorphins and dopamine, providing an internal reward. The heroes in this book are examples of this phenomenon that has occurred throughout history. As we read each heroic story, especially during these trying times, we get goosebumps that perhaps can offer some sort of comfort and hope that there are heroes, or perhaps "guardian angels" just waiting for their chance to thrive.

—JOANNE BODIN, PH.D., AWARD-WINNING AUTHOR AND POET

Pamela Warren Williams' latest book is a contemporary *Profiles in Courage*. Here is a wide-ranging, inclusive sampling of heroes, both historical and living, obscure and famous, women and men. Some are unlikely heroes, indeed! Forty-two short chapters tell their stories in both poetry and prose, a most effective combination that allows readers to discover insights that go beyond mere facts of a life. *Courage: Living from the Heart* is a fascinating read, a compelling demonstration that courage can arise in many forms and places, not limited to disasters and battlefields.

—JOHN ROCHE, AUTHOR OF *TUBBABLES* AND *JOE RIDES AGAIN*

This collection truly captures something we all recognize—past and present—and offers hope for the future. It reflects what it means to be authentically yourself and to do what is needed in the moment. Sometimes, a hero is simply an ordinary person who acts naturally, without hesitation or self-interest. They don't pause to consider the positive impact their actions may have—on those around them now or in the future—and they rarely seek credit for the progress they help inspire. As Warren Williams beautifully expresses, heroes come in many forms. What unites them is the impact they make—whether on many, a few, or even just one person. This work radiates a sense of universal love that Warren Williams embodies, and that spirit is reflected throughout this small but powerful book of art and message.

—Leo Adams, G777 Workshop Facilitator in Magick, Qabalah, Tarot and Alchemy

Courage: Living from the Heart is a book of uncommon beauty. Foremost, it is a book that illustrates the beauty of human compassion and empathy expressed within individual acts of courage. In this book Williams offers up a broad spectrum of tales of courageous individuals, between literally running into a burning building to save lives to individual, repeated actions over the course of a lifetime dedicated to enacting humane principles and values when those acts place one's own welfare at great risk. The structure of the book enhances an inherent lyricism within these acts of courage. Each story is first introduced to the reader in the context of a poem within which the author's melodic rhythms and visceral imagery add poetic profundity that prepares fertile ground for the reader to deeply connect with the accompanying narrative. These stories are certainly meant to acknowledge each person's individual tale of courage. However, the power of the book is the model of these exemplary beings in the aggregate of the poems and tales as they clearly demonstrate love for one's fellow human beings is the foundation upon which acts of courage are built, both great and small. Living from the heart is the well from which courage is drawn.

—Annie Kile creates visual art, poetry, short stories and is of course working on a novel. Her work has been published in various anthologies, most recently her poetry and collage art in *American Graveyard: A Literary Art Anthology to End Gun Violence*

I applaud Pamela Warren Williams for putting together a book of heroes, especially now, right now, with our country in crisis on so many levels. Right now I'm singing with a chorus—songs often based on the speeches and poems of heroes such as Greta Thunberg, who is one of Pamela's 42 heroes in this book! And hero she is! The heroes I sometimes most struggle with are the ones who fight against variations of how their mind works as opposed to what people call "normal". Like Thunberg, who has Asperger's, and Temple Grandin (also in this book), who has a form of Autism, there are times that heroes seem a bit off-putting. This book reminds me, as I need to be reminded on a daily basis, to stop, feel some compassion, have some empathy, and remember how tough it is for a hero to be a hero sometimes!

—Angela L. Wilson, author of *White Dan for 200*

When the world is full of worry as it is at the moment, it is easy to become engulfed by anxiety and feel as though nothing that we do matters any more. When those moments threaten, take COURAGE from this collection of prose poems from Pamela Warren Williams. Each poem, intelligent and compassionate, explores the events that transfigure ordinary people into heroes. Some you will know— Henrietta Lacks, Harvey Milk, Geronimo—others you will not; but each poem is accompanied by a back story for the person, so you need not fear that the unfamiliar names will blow past you. Their stories reach out from history and newsprint (and now Pamela's poetry collection) to reassure us that heroes are not confined to the fantastical realms of Marvel: They drive school buses, they work in the fashion industry, they captain ships, they make a difference.

—Alison Cross, author of *A Year in the Wildwood*

The great Scottish bard Dick Gaughan sang, "There are no gods and precious few heroes!". Gaughan was bemoaning the cult of Bonnie Prince Charlie, the Jacobite prince whom Gaughan accused of "running like a rabbit" away from the tragic Battle of Culloden, leaving his Highland army, "better men than him", to be slaughtered.

While many good folk might dispute Gaughan's rhetorical atheism while not endorsing hero-worship, yet all may agree that we do need heroes, historical and present, particularly in troubled times such as these.

Warren Williams gives us precious heroes, and not few of them, in this powerful collection of tribute poems.

A fine read, highly recommended!

—Bill Nevins, Poet Laureate of the Enchanted Circle, Taos New Mexico

In this poetry, in these stories, find the alchemy of Pamela Warren Williams, transforming the stuff all of us humans possess to the gold of bravery and love. Become a more caring, courageous person by reading and re-reading the words of this book.

—Tom Hester, retired statistical editor

Pamela Warren Williams set out a Herculean task: Tell the stories of nearly fifty people who exhibited extraordinary courage either in a single event or throughout their lives. And I can report without fear of contradiction she has met the challenge. Through passionate and powerful poetry and riveting prose, Warren Williams introduces the reader to a California bus driver, an environmental attorney, a South Vietnamese Air Force officer, an Olympic silver medalist, and many more. In this time of unfortunate polarization, these stories inspire us to realize there are people in this world who were and are forces for good. Warren Williams assures us this is not a definitive roster for in her preface are listed many more candidates for what I hope will be a second volume.

—Mark Fleisher, Award-winning author

Cover Images (shown left-right, top-bottom)

Haydée Santamaria

Kevin McKay

Shavarsh Karapetyan

Pia Klemp

Yevdokiya Bershanskaya and the Night Witches

Major Buang-Ly on the deck of the USS Midway

Cecil Williams and Janice Mirikitani

Mary Magdalene

Caitlyne Gonzalez

James ‘Butch’ Rosser Jr.

Harvey Milk

Temple Grandin

Sarah and Angela Grimke

Juan Velasco

Peter Norman

Robert Smalls

Robert Bilott

Fritz Sam

Henrietta Lacks

Other Works by *Pamela Warren Williams*

Hair on Fire

You Always Near, The Stewart Poems

Upward Spiral Anthology
with Shelly Barnett
Leonore Hildebrandt,
and Lynne Zotalis

Courage: Living from the Heart

Courage: Living from the Heart

Heroes Revealed

Pamela Warren Williams

Courage: Living from the Heart
Heroes Revealed

ISBN 978-1-949652-48-2
Publisher Mercury HeartLink
Silver City, New Mexico
Printed in the United States of America

Front Cover image: Heroes revealed, key on pg. vii

‘Victory Salute’ from 1968 Olympics in Mexico City pg. 3

‘Captain Klemp’ photo pg. 31

‘Sybyl Ludington on Star’ pg. 59

Monument Valley pg. 75

Author photo: 'Favorite Things' Project, Axel Contemporary, Santa Fe, NM

Mercury HeartLink: consult@heartlink.com

for just a few of my personal heroes—

Stewart Warren, Kim Webb, John Foster, Ann Lowe,
Hank Blackwell, Candida and Dennis Covington,
Belynda Webb, Bobbie Wagner, Phillip Hassrick,
Cece Stanford, Ozy Gershon, and Jean DiGregory.

We need our gods,
which is to say we need
our heroes, people who
on this plane of life
act in ways that inspire us
and help us find
our own best selves.

—Max Reif

You don't leave home
unless home
is the mouth of a shark.

—Warsan Shire,
London youth poet laureate emeritus

Whether sailing into the Aquarian age
or heading straight for Armageddon,
the work remains the same:
to quiet your mind,
open your heart,
and try to relieve the suffering around you.

—Ram Dass

Contents

Preface

In my efforts to maintain a balance of positive input, I have encountered stories of amazing heroics, both historically and in current news over the last few years of the work on this project. Please note that each story was factual in that moment and history has marched on since then. I watch out for them, now—so many more that I admire and could have included: Dora Rodriguez, Boyan Slat, Mary Ann Brown Patten, Volodymyr Zelenskyy, Mackenzie Scott, David Hogg, Bishop Mariann Budde, Gisele Pelicot, Neerja Bhanot, Todd Beamer, Mark Bingham, Roko Camaj, Mary McLeod Bethune, Grace Hopper, Welles Crother, Phillis Wheatley, Anthony Borges, Qamar Zia, Jose Gregorio, Alfred Wagener, Haym Salomon, Bob and Teresa Fletcher, Ruth Coker Burks, Kate Chopin, Marilyn Wills, Ella Gibson Hobart, Virginia Giuffre, Bette Nesmith Graham, Johanna July, bell hooks, Frances Oldham Kelsey, Eglantyne Jebb, Barbara Ledermann Rodbell, Makereti Papakura, Luisa Moreno, Lise de Baissact, Hugh Thompson Jr., Pauli Murray, Waris Dirie, Lilly Ledbetter, Dolores Huerta, Margaret Tobin Brown, Jon & Dorothea Bon Jovi, Nancy Cunard, Mary Jane Rathbun, Eunice Shriver, Joan Trumpauer Mulholland, Jud-Lynn del Rey, Howard G. Buffet, Elouise Cobell, Jamey Ruth Klassen, Ruth Coker Burks, Douglas Hegdahl, Eugene Goodman, David Gelbaum, Victoria Soto, Angélique de Coudray, Maggie Kuhn, Alexei Navalny, Branch Rickey, Jackie Robinson, Clara Lemlich, Leona Tate, Tori Amos, Riley Howell, Stacey Park Milbern, and so many everyday folks saving and improving countless lives. I admit to often weeping, reading of those who have revealed themselves as heroes, whether by a moment's selfless act or by lifestyle and strength of character. In this uncertain time, I think we need all the role models we can get. I am especially heartened by the stories of contemporary young people who are moved to heroics, perhaps indicating a shift to more generous hearts. Some of these people may not be familiar to you, or you may now see them in a new light. I invite you to explore those I mention.

This collection of stories reflects my own journey of admiration, if not my own bravery beyond my pen. You may recognize some character references from my life in southwestern New Mexico near our southern border where new heroes are often present as a counterbalance to all the pain in the area. Perhaps you will be inclined to research who they are and maybe even to learn a little Spanish. Some asylum seekers have flown and then walked from the other side of the world, some traveling over the Darién Gap between Colombia and Panama at unimaginable peril or traveling the Devil's Highway through the Arizona desert. Their bravery in the face of the unknown is legendary. My late husband, the poet and publisher, Stewart S. Warren, is referred to in my writing and I credit him with encouraging the inception of these stories. There are tales of bravery, ingenuity in the face of resistance, and resulting transformations. The optimist in me is uplifted to know of all those working for a better, kinder future on a nurtured planet. You will see opportunities to dive deeper into someone's story and possibly contribute to that work or become more involved. May this writing help to reveal ways to connect more deeply with others on this journey and with our own higher selves.

I ask forbearance for any inaccuracies in either historic stories or more current events. My lens is as a poet, not a researcher. I invite your further inquiry.

Formatted with a background story of each hero, prefaced by a poem honoring their courage, you may choose to read their story first, or my preferred pattern, poem first to pique your interest and see what it evokes, much like reading a Tarot card. Historical figures, war heroes, bold women surmounting assumed roles, assorted cultures and races appearing in no particular order. You are encouraged to pass this book along after reading, to inspire further uplifting and connection.

All love and reverence,
Pamela Warren Williams
Silver City, New Mexico
2026

Introduction

There are times in our homo-sapiens history when our evolution lags well behind our de-evolution. It is during these cycles when heroes . . . true heroes show up. Pamela has done the same. Not only has she carefully chosen her heroic humans and their stories with meticulous care, but she also has "stood in her stirrups" with an artist's and hero's conviction.

Pamela is a remarkable publisher, generous as an "ambassador for the words and the truth told" as she guides her authors toward their own genius. More importantly, she is a remarkable poet, a "role model for persuasion as well as courageous audacity." Her wordsmithing is likened to her silversmithing, communicating with the metal of her words in order to create soulful images as a "purveyor of endless magic."

A few more samplings of her word art found in this exceptional work include "the children of her tribe were paid in peach cobbler" and "that bullet blew the door wide open." These poems underscore the heroes' stories that can only find their images through Pamela's soulful approach to our occupation of the planet. Her words reflect her deep conviction of the higher self and her unwavering belief in kindness. Her timely and brilliant construct of *Courage: Living from the Heart* has arrived exactly when we need it so very much in these dystopian and somewhat unkind times. She reminds us of our critical responsibility to be kind, generous, honest and in terms of these traits, to not leave feelings unsaid.

We are all in need of Pamela's heroes and her lovely words. As she underscores in one of her poetic works of art in this astounding manuscript, she reminds us to have "fearless opinions, fearless generosity."

I urge all of you and those within your circle to immerse yourselves in the message, beauty and incredible hope of this amazing book and get to know just a portion of the warmth and courage of Pamela Warren Williams. She is clearly a much-needed hero and for me, a dear and valued friend. Whether you have your hero, or are in search of one, Pamela will help you celebrate the ones you have or help you find one! I wish for all of you the blessing of this remarkable writer's craft, her stunning talent, and her courageous generosity. May you give Pamela permission to accompany you on your journey and purpose; she has surely reciprocated in *Courage: Living from the Heart.*

—Hank Blackwell, author of *Silver Chain, Closer to the Door, LeapYear: Rising on Invisible Wings,* and editor for *A Wind Blows Through Us: A Festival of New Mexico Poetry* from New Mexico Men's Wellness

Heroes Revealed

Powerfully Invisible

Ultimately, it was his own thought
to leave that third podium bare
on the commemorative bronze monument.
An opportunity for all
to climb up there and imagine themselves
a hero in solidarity with the Civil Rights movement.
Peter Norman lived with the weight
of apartheid discrimination
in his own Australia and
ultimately challenged that system alone.

Listening to John Carlos and Tommie Smith
planning their rebellious gesture, with love for justice,
he quietly asked for one of the badges
of the Olympic Project for Human Rights,
to share in their statement.
Intuitively, another activist surrendered his own.
Only one shared pair of the famous black gloves,
and an unassuming white man, so much smaller
in stature, co-creating that historic moment.
With Bobby and Martin, so recently taken
from the front lines.

Now, fifty years later, Norman's record
remains untouched,
while ostracized and discriminated against
ever afterward.
His refusal to condemn his fellow athletes
in exchange for a pardon
by the system that shunned him
at such a cost to his own career,
defined who he was.
In the end, his friends, the two fastest men in America
carried Peter Norman home.

Peter Norman—his story

Those of a certain age all seem to remember the 1968 Olympics in Mexico City, for that seminal moment in the history of protests, in a time of rising consciousness of racial inequality. The three 200-meter sprint medal winners, two from the U.S., included a diminutive force from Australia named Peter Norman. It was his observation that they only needed one glove each—there was only one pair. He stood proudly with John Carlos and Tommie Smith as they raised their fists, wearing one of the badges of the Olympic Project for Human Rights.

All Indigenous peoples in Australia could vote for the first time in 1965; there was a referendum that all Indigenous peoples to be counted in the Census for the first time in 1967; and the forced removal of children was a policy still taking place. And for his solidarity, he spent the rest of his life ostracized in his native country, struggling to find work, his family penalized along with him. After his silver medal, he qualified eighteen more times for the next Olympics, denied entrance to compete by his own government. The subsequent life size bronze statue, now at San Jose State (Carlos and Smith's alma mater, in CA), honors the moment with America's two heroes and an empty platform, offering the opportunity to visualize oneself a hero. Peter Norman died of a heart attack in 2006, with Smith and Carlos as his pall bearers. In 2008, Norman's nephew produced a documentary about Peter, called *Salute*. In 2012, Australian parliament formally apologized for the country's failure to fully recognize his powerful, inspirational role in furthering racial equality in Australia.

1
2
3

Goyahkla

Following Geronimo's tracks,
while certain that he left none.

Master of subterfuge,
sleight of hand and cunning,
this mystic, medicine man.

His knowing of the terrain secured
over a quarter century's freedom.
Evasion, again and again.
Soldiers' coats on the soap yucca;
more than a worthy obstacle
to having all this land.

Finally pursued by a fourth of the
standing army and 3000 Mexicans.

Word—that no bullet could touch him,
his arrows guided.

Proud defender of the Chiricahuas
and what was theirs.

He would not be subjected,
rejecting hollow promises.

What if your family were slaughtered
in your absence. Or your land
donated despite all your ancestors.

Geronimo—his story

The 1848 signing of the treaty ending the Mexican American War, ceded 55% of Mexico's land to the US, including Apache homeland of centuries. Then in 1854, the US paid Mexico with the Gadsden Purchase for 29,670 square miles to become part of Arizona and New Mexico—the rest of Chiricahua Apache territory. While Geronimo was away on a trading trip in 1851, Mexican soldiers attacked his family's camp, murdering Geronimo's wife, Alope, their three children, and his mother. Over the next few decades, the U.S. government tried to coax Geronimo and his followers onto reservations, but they escaped each time, avoiding recapture. The U.S. military and elected officials faced years of humiliation as the news of his ability to evade them made national headlines. Among the Chiricahua, he was better known for his skills as a shaman, or medicine man, credited with a variety of supernatural powers including the ability to heal the sick, slow time, avoid bullets, bring on rainstorms and witness events over great distances. His ancestral knowledge of the terrain enabled him and his warriors with women and children in tow to travel as much as seventy miles a day through the desert.

In 1886, Geronimo finally agreed to surrender on the condition that he and his people would be able to return to their beloved homelands. He was with seventeen of his bravest warriors, and a handful of women and children. But Geronimo never saw home again. Initially, they were transported to Fort Pickens, Florida, then Alabama, and finally imprisoned at Fort Sill, Oklahoma. In Florida, the government placed their children at Carlisle Indian Industrial School in Pennsylvania where a third of them died at the notoriously inhumane boarding school. He was the last Native American leader to formally surrender to the U.S. military, spending his last twenty-three years a prisoner of war. The government's failure to understand the importance of tribal identity played a key role in the tragedy of the Apache wars.

The Ministry of Perros Bravos Barrio

Her birth only rumored.
Macon Georgia a possibility.
Stories of her journey
laden with holes and mysteries.
The known astounding in its breadth.
Who else could claim this array of skills?
A curandera. Strong woman for any era.
In this town that continues its siren call
to so many creatives and givers,
she knew how to create sovereignty,
for herself and all those disadvantaged.
Benefactor with bread and milk and property,
healer, birther, builder,
sometimes deputized, often revered.

The children of her tribe
were paid in peach cobbler.
Entrusted with the future of some
for a fee of two dollars
after midnight on Saturday.

Her world apotropaic,
while deeply rooted in daily realities
and obvious faith.
Surrounded by taxidermy, potions,
doll heads and her enigmatic library,
she kept counsel with a raven.
Her regal presence as a savvy businesswoman
left memories of her shrewd dealings
with funds stashed under that long black skirt.
At ninety-seven, she took her sister on
a cruise to the Bahamas.

Rebecca Brewer—her story

Her astonishing life spanning a century, from 1868 to 1969, rumored to be the child of slaves, her legacy radiates outward from her community roots in an area of Silver City, NM now known as Brewer Hill. Initially settling there in 1900 as one of few African American residents, she bought up property and sold parcels cheaply so that more people could own homes—particularly those unable to acquire bank loans such as the Chinese, Hispanics, and African Americans. She gave land for the neighborhood Baptist Church, while acting as a midwife, curandera, and sheriff's deputy, also working as construction foreman for Elizabeth Warren, another local pioneer, whose construction company had all female bosses. Stories abound of her healing prowess, with speculation that she offered abortions. At one time, her house burned in the night. All of the neighborhood children rushed in their pajamas to drag her mattress into the street, knowing that was where she kept her money. She told fortunes for two dollars, usually after midnight on Saturdays. Clearly, she changed the trajectory of the lives of many.

Bus 963 from Paradise

I knew better than to click on that link.
On the day I had buried your pipe bag
as instructed. A tender melancholy lingering.
I could say that from your hospice bed,
you were not mindful as usual of the work required.
Your gentle gratitude was ever present, of my efforts, then.

Compelled to complete that task,
as I doubtfully carried Papaw's pick and shovel up our rocky hill.
A couple of those rocks the size of your head.
Lots of stopping for breath.
Never a better time, after last night's downpour.
An apology that I kept the native rattle—
too precious to surrender.

And that ill-advised link? I had adjourned
to my realm of technology, thinking to
balance the scales with a bit of work. But
an article appeared, sharing the valor of the
bus driver who rescued twenty-two children
from the Paradise fire along with two teachers
in a harrowing five-hour journey to safety.
Driving through the burning destruction,
challenged by gridlock and fears.
One remaining resident offered water.
The driver instructed: 'Rip my undershirt into
twenty-five squares and soak them for
filters to breathe through.' Each bigger child
seated with a smaller one to encourage.

At some point, the driver realized that he was
witnessing the demise of his town.
Hand holding and prayers.

And such a travesty
that the driver was paid eleven dollars an hour.
What was that fourteen-hour day worth?
My own day now humbly pallid in its turn.

Kevin McKay—his story

An unassuming forty-one-year-old man, in the role of elementary school bus driver for only a few months, became a savior for a bus load of children whose parents were unable to reach the school, with a thousand fires racing near in Paradise, California. He had just dropped the children off for their day at school, when it became obvious that someone needed to evacuate the remaining twenty-two children and two teachers. His own family had already been evacuated, allowing his full concentration on his mission. He had already learned that his home was lost to the fire. Thus, his bus began an unimaginable five-hour journey through darkness, choking smoke, and flames. At one point he realized that he was watching the decimation of Paradise. Seeing that some of the children were nearly passing out from smoke and carbon monoxide, he finally acquired a single bottle of water from a young man also stuck in the gridlocked traffic. He instructed the teachers to tear up his undershirt to soak the pieces for makeshift respirators for everyone.

At one point, the bus was sideswiped in the mayhem of traffic. The local police were attempting to facilitate the gridlock of fleeing traffic, but the massive exodus had overwhelmed them. They insisted on trying to direct Kevin's bus down a narrow rural road that he knew had brush and branches encroaching from both sides, surely impassable by then. Another school employee following in his truck, blocked the road to allow Kevin to follow his instincts to safety. I was unable to find any further background on Kevin McKay, who appeared suddenly as a hero. Sometimes, one simply rises to the demands of the moment.

Wonder as an Offering

Anonymous purveyor of boundless magic.
In visual, functional, and edible arenas.

This mutable sorceress,
adept despite obstacles
unfathomable to most of us mortals.

Raw truths released with all humility
to Patreon patrons and to
all of us who can only marvel at
such courage and fortitude,
sworn to withhold advice,
but to only hold space
and send virtual hugs.

The phrase, against all odds is evident.
What would we each offer from this bed
of pain and list of challenges?
Such a warrior, a rare and precious gift
to us all, in this warm and creative
embrace of life, whatever it may bring.

The Wondersmith—her story

Ethereal and minutely detailed tea sets are not yet for sale, with plans for them afoot and a firm belief that for her, art is not a commodity. The equally astounding and meticulous culinary delights come from hand foraged herbs— also previous training for that. There are free events in fairytale settings for patrons, now accessed through Patreon.

The Wondersmith, with an art and design background, lives in the Pacific Northwest, fearlessly sparring with the ongoing obstacles of her chronic medical conditions which prohibit any sustenance other than what comes through a picc line with a port in her chest. Much time must be spent on medical access and advocacy. There are debilitating days and sometimes severe pain for weeks, triumphing over that pain only through focus on emerging creativity on a hospital bed table. Her fertile imagination conjures projects such as little memory bowls with glaze created from ash from the homes of those whose property was lost in the Paradise fire and another offering for losses in the Maui fire. Bringing wonder to as many of us as possible, her mission. Having grown up in the Idaho backcountry, she lives her deep connection with the natural world, gifting us with its endless beauty and solace, along with wondrous recipes for her creations, her name irrelevant. Bold proof demonstrated that determination and creativity can triumph over disability. https://www.misswondersmith.com

"I don't make art for commerce. I make it for connection"

—The Wondersmith

Twenty-Five Seconds per Life

In the final one of his selfless heroic feats
Shavarsh Karapetyan dove into
cold murky lake water.
Thirty-Five feet down,
the finswimming champion kicked out
a window of the wrecked streetcar,
pulling thirty-seven to safety
one at a time.

Hospitalized for a month with the victims,
undeterred from his passion,
he managed to acquire the last
of his collection of gold medals,
no stranger to setting records.

Neither a stranger to quick thinking,
he had rescued another busload of people
when an unattended bus began rolling
towards a mountain gorge.
Breaking down the partition,
he steered them all to safety.

Later, among the first into
a burning sports arena,
Shavarsh says,
"Our whole lives, we all owe everything to each other,"

An asteroid, named in his honor,
just a piece of his legacy.

Shavarsh Karapetyan—his story

Athletically gifted, a total of thirty-seven gold medals to his credit, with eleven world records, the Armenian finswimming champion also made numerous humanitarian rescues, finally at the cost of his stamina and career after his dramatic rescue of the passengers on a wrecked and submerged streetcar. For a month afterward, he fought for his life with double pneumonia and septic fever. Retiring at age twenty-four, he held seventeen world championship titles, thirteen European championship titles and seven Soviet championship titles in underwater swimming. Despite becoming an urban legend, the Soviet press keeps his heroics unknown, not wanting to publicize such accidents. Six years later, upon release of an article about his rescue, he received tens of thousands of letters of appreciation.

Having since carried the Olympic torch, he now heads a foundation in his name and coaches his son in swimming, hoping for a continuation of his legacy of achievement. His lifetime of giving speaks loudly of that.

Seduction

The power of a romantic story . . .
At over six carats
and carrying the mystique
of the Atocha,
the ring will no doubt do
Sotheby's and Mel Fisher proud.

Mitzi realizes the value of
the background story.
In lieu of a check,
the flash of that emerald may lure
a higher bid.

At this age, we reevaluate what matters.
Languishing for four hundred years,
costing lives and millions
over sixteen years of searching.

Finally, the gleam of gold doubloons
pointed the way.
Chicken farmers paved the path
to this success.

Now Mitzi pays it forward,
planning to fund a shelter
in Ukraine to protect
the vulnerable from trafficking,
supporting such resilience
as she saw there.

Mitzi Perdue—Her Story

The 1622 shipwreck of the *Nuestra Senora de Atocha* cost Spain 180,000 gold coins, 24 tons of Bolivian silver, 125 bars of gold bullion, and 70 pounds of rough-cut emeralds—a recovered value of $400 million worth of treasure. It sank near Key West, in a hurricane. The treasure hunter, Mel Fisher was aided in his years of searching for the *Atocha* by his close friend, Frank Perdue, who shared his history of chicken farming. When Mel and his team located the *Atocha*, Perdue received a share of the treasure, mostly donated to the Smithsonian. He kept one emerald to have an engagement ring made for Mitzi, who then became his wife. Thrilled by its history, she wore the ring until Frank's death in 2005, when she put it away in her safe.

Mitzi traveled to Ukraine earlier this year to learn more about human trafficking, a subject that she writes about for Psychology Today. Because of an air raid threat, she spent her first night in Kyiv in a bomb shelter, relayed as one of the most consequential experiences of her life. At eighty-one, she realized that given the historical significance of the emerald, it gave her the most leverage to lessen suffering for more people. Despite Sotheby's estimate of $70k, Mitzi's ring sold for $1.2 million. On her website, https://mitziperdue.com/, the human rights activist, who also happens to be the heiress to the Sheraton Hotels fortune, explained that proceeds from the sale will purchase warm clothes, flashlights, generators, and other items requested by the Mayors of Lviv and Kyiv. Some funds will rehab buildings on the Ukrainian border, where women can be counseled before they cross.

"Human traffickers prey on the vulnerable," she wrote, *"and during the Ukraine war, traffickers lurk on Ukraine's borders, targeting women and children. The goal is to keep them from making a decision that may cost them their lives."*

"To Die for the Country is to Live Forever"

Led by her convictions, resolutely against dictatorship,
only strengthened by attempts at gory intimidation.
Haydee Santamaria stood for justice despite the risks,
the suffering, the losses, her own and for all.

Lesser known, but perhaps the most influential figure
in the Cuban revolution.
A friend to Che and Fidel,
smuggler and disseminator of the manifesto,
present for every step to victory and beyond.

Introduced at a young age to the writing
of the intellectual revolutionary hero, Jose Marti,
adept at handling both words and weaponry
as the need arose.

Redefined through her commitment to change and equality,
Castro 's choice to found the Casa,
a haven for creative intellect and culture,
giving voice to all Latin American dissidents,
a beacon for connecting all those suffering oppression.
Triumphant in that for so many years.

Haydée Santamaria—her story

Considered one of the most prominent heroines of the Cuban Revolution, Haydée was involved from the first assault in 1953, having been drawn into the conflict through her brother and his associates, who included Fidel Castro. She was among the few involved for the duration. From the beginning, she smuggled weapons and participated in organizing, as well as being in guerrilla forces. As a child, she had been exposed to the writings of many strong and rebellious figures including that of the intellectual revolutionary hero, Jose Marti, national symbol of Cuban independence. Despite her imprisonment after the Moncada assault, in which she was tortured and shown one of her brother's eyes and the mangled testicle of her fiancé, she responded, "If you did that to them and they didn't talk, much less will I." They were both subsequently killed, and she rose resolutely to a leadership role, to be maintained until her death despite the challenges of her resulting depression over her losses.

After her release from prison she helped to found the 26th of July Movement, joining the guerrilla forces led by Fidel Castro and Che Guevara. Then at the end of the revolution, she was tagged by Castro to found the cultural institute Casa de las Americas, and she acted as its director for two decades. It was a bold institute, giving voice to the work of Latin American dissidents, and continuing that work today. In addition to literature, the institution brought innovative music, painting and theatre to the Cuban people. Haydée Santamaría's unique role within the Casa de las Americas allowed her to practice internationalism in the face of the U. S. embargo against Cuba, creating a safe container for artists and intellectuals from around the world to meet and collaborate and giving a voice to countless bold women around the globe.

Immortality

In the guise of a country schoolteacher
A one room school in up-holler Kentucky
Inception of his journey,
younger and smaller than some pupils
to whom he had to prove his mettle.
Challenged from all sides,
opposition including officials
unable to write
their own names.

Jesse Stuart altered systems
and the course of an infinite number of lives
So many teachers he trained
in the path of inspiration and play,
from barefoot ruffians to
teachers themselves.

An enduring legacy
embracing Jesse's joy
and determination.
His collection of international awards
and status as poet laureate
extraneous to his path.

Jesse Stuart—his story

Humble son of a railroad man, of parents who respected the value of the education they didn't have, Jesse managed to snag a teaching job at age seventeen. He bucked many traditions in place, to instill joy and ambition in generations of rural Kentucky youth, subsequently becoming principal, superintendent, special consultant and international lecturer. A bestselling and award-winning writer, he produced over sixty volumes of poetry, novels, and 460 short stories, immortalizing his beloved hill country. He was elected Kentucky poet laureate in 1954.

His autobiographical book, *The Thread that Runs So True* (1949), was hailed by the president of the National Education Association as the finest book on education in fifty years. His collection of sonnets, *Man with a Bull-tongue Plow*, created a sensation when published in 1934 and established Jesse Stuart as a major American writer. Its origins were in the Appalachian mountains of Kentucky where young Stuart worked a fifty-acre farm and yet managed to find time to write down the poems that burned in him. Kentucky comes to life in each line: sunlight on green fields, clean winds blowing through corn, stars above the mountains, all tenderly recorded. Dozens of dramas and scores of characters inhabit the pages. The Nation's critics hailed *Man with a Bull-Tongue Plow* as an outstanding American poetic work, and anointed its author to the company of Burns, Housman, Masters, and Frost. Time has not altered this verdict. *Man with a Bull-Tongue Plow* embodies the spirit and the essence of poetry. Stuart later became a far-sighted conservationist, donating over 700 acres of his land in W-Hollow to the Kentucky Nature Preserves System in 1980.

4Kinship

Forty years a fashion industry executive,
Amy Denet Deal next put her accrued skills to work
as a preservationist for her Dinè community,
its children, and its traditions,
one ghost bead at a time.

Honoring homeland.
Reinvesting profit in funding shelters and skateparks.
Her business vision waylaid by Covid,
the Pandemic ultimately designated her a hero.

Pivoting, her space becoming a command center,
she raised nearly a million dollars,
provided for forty-two thousand tribal children,
funding over a million meals and over a million PPE boxes.
Embracing her reconnection with home.

Sharing honor with Fauci, she stands for integrity,
collaboration, and care, now a driving force for the people.
There will be a strategic action plan in Santa Fe
supporting the indigenous.

Denet Deal's work a vessel for respect and humility,
healing and lessons for us all.

Amy Denet Deal—her story

As Anthony Fauci was receiving his lifetime achievement award in 2021, Amy Denet Deal was designated Trailblazer of the year. Having done her homework in Intertribal relations, as well as executive diplomacy, she is skilled in the care and integrity required to fundraise and collaborate with grace. She made a fundraising concert with Jewel happen to fund forty-two thousand care boxes for Dinè children (the proper tribal name for the 'Navajo' people). Her work funded a shelter for Dinè domestic abuse survivors and contributed significantly to helping many in her tribal community to survive the challenges of Covid, including lack of water and food. Adopted and raised in distant Indiana, she speaks gently of the moment she entered a room filled with people who looked like her, fulfilling that unnamed longing for home. A connector at heart, she bridged generations in their artistic skills and collaborations, showing the work of edgy younger artists without any other platform in Santa Fe, as they incorporated the techniques of their elders. Promoting upcycling, claiming the role of preservationist, Denet Deal stands firmly in that juxtaposition between the past and future, now launching Indigenous Futures 4EVER foundation to support young Native people in the creative arts, outdoor recreation, and sustainability.

Commander

Born into slavery.
He piloted his way to freedom,
giving a hand and paving the path
for so many others.
Offering the proper signals,
face hidden by the captain's
signature straw boater hat,
he bluffed his way,
through Charleston harbor
to the safety of the U. S. blockade
blessing them with arms and secrets.

He demonstrated to Lincoln the gifts
of African American soldiers
in the Union army.
Role model for persuasion,
as well as courageous audacity.
Attaining fitting rank, himself.

Reconstruction as an alchemical action.
The Carolina legislature
offered a fresh arena for change.
The first free and compulsory schools
came from his determination.
A worthy success story
for any history book.
His great-great grandson speaks
of the endowment of expectations
that come with such a legacy.

Robert Smalls—his story

Born into slavery in the low-country Gullah culture, he was sent to Charleston, South Carolina as a laborer at age twelve. Finding work on the docks, he worked his way up to the position of wheelman, slaves not permitted to captain. In 1862, he commandeered a Confederate transport ship, manned by slaves, and sailed through the Confederate-controlled harbor and surrounding blockade to the Union enclave at Beaufort-Port Royal-Hilton Head, where it became a Union warship. This action, his continued bravery, and his persuasion led President Abraham Lincoln to accept African American soldiers into the Union Army. The entire crew and their families were granted their freedom.

Witness' account of the ship's approach to the navy fleet.: "Just as No. 3 port gun was being elevated, someone cried out, 'I see something that looks like a white flag,' and true enough there was something flying on the steamer that would have been white by application of soap and water. As she neared us, we looked in vain for the face of a white man. When they discovered that we would not fire on them, there was a rush of contrabands out on her deck, some dancing, some singing, whistling, jumping, and others stood looking towards Fort Sumter, and muttering all sorts of maledictions against it, and 'de heart of de South,' generally. As the steamer came near, and under the stern of the *Onward*, one of the Colored men stepped forward, and taking off his hat, shouted, 'Good morning, sir! I've brought you some of the old United States guns, sir!" That man was Robert Smalls.

Smalls subsequently went on to be a successful businessman and longtime congressman, serving both houses of the South Carolina legislature, credited with early free compulsory schools in his state, and active in passing the Civil Rights bill.

Disparity for a Ten-year-old

Beginning even younger now.
Sadly not uncommon
for a ten-year-old child to become an advocate.
Having lost friends to the pervasive violence, she
leaves the safety of her stuffed animals and her
mother's side to step up and speak
even in Washington
about the inaction of the Uvalde police.
She is compared to that bronze girl,
facing off the charging bull.
But this is far more insidious.
The crime that we do not protect our children . . .

She knows the names of all the Parkland victims
and so much more
that it is so wrong for her to know.
Despite the training wheels
still on her bike,
she knows about bullet-proof backpacks
and lives with the dichotomy of
Bad Bunny TikToks and gun control stats.

As with so many of her peers, ptsd-style
flashbacks assail her. Toddler lullabies suffice.
Nightmares commonplace,
a grief workshop not enough.
Meeting Beto brought some joy
in an increasingly scary world
where trust in the police has been outgrown.
But then a teen survivor from another shooting

reaches out with loving comfort.

Caitlyne Gonzalez—her story

Tragically, Caitlyne, at age ten, became the voice for her classmates who were murdered in Uvalde, Texas in the school shooting on May 24, 2022. There were a total of nineteen children and two teachers who lost their lives in one of so many such shootings—all while nearly 400 officers from multiple agencies spent seventy-seven minutes listening to the shooter shooting, in direct violation of ‘active shooter protocol’. Writing her own speeches with an adult eloquence, she has spoken about fear and death and the need for assault weapon bans, in front of her school board and U.S. senators in Washington—on her tiptoes.

She spends a great deal of her time visiting the graves of her friends and studying online information from other school shooting survivors, to be better informed for future appearances at rallies and governmental meetings. Feeling most unsafe at night, she remains too anxious and even panicked over being alone, disrupting family life for her little sister and parents. The grief counseling available to her has been insufficient and ineffective. As of October 24, 2022, there were 257 shootings on school campuses, causing mental health challenges for countless survivors.

The Primacy of Humility

A universe ablaze with light, his default view.
A perspective deep within.

Denying the dualistic divorce of his inheritance.

Relishing communion with the earth.
Glory and suffering inseparable.

The ultimate address of matter offering doctrinal threat
enough to exile him from influence.

Within, rather than opposed to.

The Oneness of interrelatedness.

Pierre Teilhard de Chardin—his story

French scientist, Jesuit priest, and mystic, Teilhard was born in 1881, managing to retain his childhood wonder at the light in the world, despite his Catholic upbringing. 'At the heart of matter is the heart of God,' he believed. Rejecting the dualism of separated spirit and matter, he found God within all things, inclusive of war and pain, bucking the church doctrine. When he wrote a prayer addressing matter, it was too much for his church superiors, who saw him threatening the foundations of church theology. In 1926 the Vatican forbade Teilhard from any teaching or from writing theology and exiled him to China on an archaeological project.

As his wisdom deepened, he told of how, after harnessing all of the earth's energies, we would ultimately learn to manage the greatest energy of love in the same way. He was then exiled to the outpost of the U.S. He called the lesson of living from the sacred ground of all life, rather than a place of perceived superiority, the "primacy of humility." He was finally prompted to sign over all of his vast body of writings to his assistant, Jeanne Mortier, who released them a year after his death. It was then forbidden by the Vatican for his writings to be in any church libraries or educational institutions.

"No truth has ever been conquered by repression."
—Teilhard

Captain Klemp Refutes Hypocrisy

There's talk of a safe harbor,
of what a humanitarian award is worth.
Unshakeable leadership.
It's been suggested that we cast
all medals into spearheads
for the revolution.
Say their names:
Pia Klemp. Carola Rackete.
Each day I tally more chronicles
of emerging warriors like these,
making their mark   making things right.
Would *you* give twenty years,
for those thousands of lives?

Oh, you don't know their stories?
These are women in their thirties,
German-born boat captains,
rescuing those displaced, and
fleeing unspeakable horrors,
from drowning in the Mediterranean.
By their own moral compass.
Believing that at sea,
we are all just people.

We already know the narrative.
You haven't seen their photos?
Strong smart women
of incredible beauty in their conviction.
They are not the first.
Just now, other captains
continue to await suspended justice
for similar rescues.

Likely the first women though,
in this tradition of those
bucking the bureaucracy.
We must not let it stop—ever.

Pia Klemp— her story

In refusing the proffered medal from the mayor of Paris, here's Pia's statement:

"Madame Hidalgo, you want to award me a medal for my solitarian action in the Mediterranean Sea, because of our crews' work to rescue migrants from difficult conditions on a daily basis. At the same time, your police are stealing blankets from people that you force to live on the streets, while you raid protests and criminalize people that are standing up for rights of migrants and asylum seekers. You want to give me a medal for actions that you fight in your own ramparts. I am sure you won't be surprised that I decline the Medaille Grand Vermeil."

Obviously, a woman of strong convictions, Pia Klemp has a background as a ship captain, animal and human rights activist, author, and biologist, among other attributes. Beginning in 2015, she began to participate in migrant rescue in the Mediterranean Sea, commanding ships there. Her ships rescued around fourteen thousand migrants from drowning. She is now awaiting trial, facing charges by the Italian government of aiding illegal immigration, that could result in twenty years in prison. Earlier this year, a boat of Turkish and Afghani refugees wrecked just off the rocky southern shore of Italy, resulting in dozens more deaths.

Sea-Watch

Dark Waters

Ultimately, all of us gifted with Teflon infusions.
Forever chemicals.   Forever.
It took the lives of over a hundred and fifty
of Wilbur's cattle as a wake-up call.
And finally the lives of Wilbur and Sandy.
So many others with an array of cancers.
The peril of a company town.
PFOA and PFAS dumped near Wilbur's farm.
Foam in the water,
downstream from DuPont's denial.
That sixty-six acres sold for landfill . . .

Twenty years to the truth.
Unregulated, still,
until Joe Biden's restriction in 2024.
In the blood of Atlantic salmon
and Alaskan polar bears,
and every being in between.
West Virginia simply a focal point.

And Rob Bilott's dedication to
accountability . . .

"It just felt like the right thing to do."

Robert Bilott—his story

Rob was a corporate defense attorney, expert in environmental law, when his grandmother's friend Wilbur Tennant reached out about his mysteriously dying cattle—over half of his herd of three hundred in two years, with obvious maladies apparently caused by water dumped into his creek from the landfill on the 66 acres his family had sold to DuPont. Rob had played on the Tennant farm near Parkersburg, West Virginia as a child. Now, in 1998, all of the area wildlife was dying, with scavengers unwilling to touch the carcasses. Wilbur shot videos of dead animals, of his autopsies, and of the foamy crusty surface of his creek.

Despite Rob's position representing large corporate clients, he took on Wilbur's case, poring over in excess of 110,000 pages of unorganized evidence, delivered by DuPont, per court order. His research revealed that DuPont had known the dangers of the chemical PFOA (perfluorooctanoic acid) used in manufacturing Teflon, since their first purchase in 1951, defying specific instructions for disposal. Hundreds of thousands of pounds of PFOA were pumped into the Ohio River, lacing the water table supplying drinking water. By the late '80's DuPont knew of resultant testicular, pancreatic, liver, and prostate cancers, having done their own lab tests. But PFOA products made DuPont over $1 billion in annual profit. By 1990, DuPont had dumped over 7K tons of PFOA sludge into the Tennant landfill. Ultimately, Rob got the Tennants a settlement and then began a class action suit, with a nearly thousand-page brief sent to every regulatory agency including the EPA and the U.S. attorney general. He became a threat to the whole unregulated flouropolymers industry. After seven years of mandated study, DuPont agreed to a 'probable link' and a replacement product that degrades more quickly. Bilott writes an annual letter to the EPA urging further regulation while he continues to try cases from the class action suit & sues other makers and users of PFOA's.

House on Fire

Greta points out that our house is on fire.
We must treat this crisis as a crisis.
I'm dismayed to see that she's growing up.
She looks older than when I saw her last and
is more poised than many twice her age.
She was already wiser than so many of us.
She says that her expression should not need
explanation. Why is it not obvious to all?
One hundred weeks. The first protest at
parliament, alone. Now millions show up.
Awarded Portuguese humanitarian glory
of over a million euros. All to be donated.
Are any of the greedy noting this example?

On the back side of my own journey, I've lost
my great love. Such a blip on the larger
screen. Can I yet find that reason for my now?
For remaining to continue the work? Well,
first, to clarify what the work is. So much
need for our focus on love interwoven
with hope and faith.   And Time.   Now.

Greta Thunberg—her story

Having first learned of climate change at the age of eight, Greta Thunberg became a vegan and refused to travel by plane. She then persuaded her parents to make lifestyle changes as well. By age sixteen, after three weeks of daily appearances, her solo weekly protest outside of the Swedish parliament had inspired hundreds of thousands of students worldwide to join her in striking. She has spoken at the World Economic Forum in Switzerland, as well as before the legislatures of Italy, France, the U.K. and the U.S. She traveled to the U.S. on an emissions-free yacht. After that speech, millions of protesters marched in climate strikes in over 163 countries. Greta advocates that we must all surrender the belief that politicians will work for climate change, since they have betrayed that trust repeatedly. Leaders from mayors to presidents have been persuaded by this forceful presence to make commitments to climate change. She was compared to Joan of Arc by Margaret Atwood. In 2019, she was named Time magazine Person of the Year.

Having been diagnosed with Asperger's, she is also credited with raising awareness and inspiring those with the disorder. While recognizing it's resulting limitations, she recognizes its advantages, in her ability to focus, for example, referring to it as her superpower.

Without Hesitation

Not his job and not his family.
But someone's family
could have been in there,
he pointed out.
There was no hesitation
in his actions,
only the grace of asking
if his passenger minded
his stopping
for momentary heroics.

He saved a life or two.
His wife surely found him out,
whether she smelled smoke on him or not.
Perhaps when the Tesla was delivered.
By the time the writer/passenger had landed,
Thousands knew.
She said, "I think this gave
a lot of people hope.
This is something so pure
and so good,
and it really pierces through
all the noise."
As a bonus, she made her flight.

And she got him that book deal. No doubt
there were some heroes in those stories.

Fritz Sam—his story

A hero may emerge suddenly from an ordinary day at work. Fritz Sam is an Uber driver in Brooklyn. His second fare for the day was a woman flying out of La Guardia to a writers' conference. Upon seeing a number of people milling in the street in front of a brownstone, Sam slowed enough to notice flames shooting from an upper story window with no fire personnel in evidence. He asked his passenger if they could stop to help and she replied, "Of course." She later elaborated that a missed flight would be no contest in comparison to someone's flaming home.

Sam rushed from his car without hesitation, tossing his cell phone to a bystander on the way. No one seemed to know if there was anyone still in the building. Pounding up the interior stairs, he passed one man who was on the way to a lower level to retrieve something. Then at the top of the staircase, he met a disoriented woman who was resistant to coming down with him, but who finally acquiesced. He then went back in to locate the man and convinced him of the value of his life beyond any belongings. As they emerged from the building, he noticed that someone had moved his car to allow the firetrucks access on the narrow street.

Resuming the ride to La Guardia, Sam inquired about smelling too much like smoke, not wanting to offend or for his wife to know what he had done. His rider learned that he hoped to publish a children's book with his two daughters, and she offered to help him to make that dream a reality. Meanwhile, Uber has provided Mr. Sam with a Tesla for his use for the next year.

Kaze

Dispensing dignity
such worthy work
along with spreading awareness
offering hope
and directions to services.
Referred to as practical caring.

Skyrocketing numbers
on those city streets.
Fallout of our crumbling economy
and fractured healthcare system.

Knowing where the teens gather
to protect one another from so much.
Don't give up.
Don't.   Give.   Up.

Amazon gift cards as currency.
McDonald's bringing simple joy,
warmth, safety, fries and coffee,
and a bathroom to clean up in.

Mylar blankets rejected,
tainted by incarceration.
What about those plastic ponchos
to replace soggy cardboard bedding?

This bold ministry
by an octogenarian warrior
Native consciousness
of our universal kinship.
Man-made knee and Divine heart.

Gramma to some.
Hero to countless others.
The gift of just listening.

Kaze Gadway —her story

From southern roots, with street smarts gleaned from time in Chicago, Kaze first found community with the Episcopals, teaching for fifty years and as a youth minister and community organizer in developing countries and on native reservations. She has spent time teaching and mentoring in Mumbai, Zambia, Peru, Ethiopia, Kenya, and numerous other countries, having worked with the Australian Aboriginals, and working with Richard Rohr. For many years her focus has been on emerging leaders in the Native American community, leaving a new generation of empowered youth in her wake, strong in integrity and living their beliefs as she continues to demonstrate. An advocate for resources, she has modeled self-advocacy along the way. Giving voice and encouraging the voices of youth show up in her firm grasp of social media and the power of a well written blog or moving Facebook post.

Kaze has called her encounter with asylum seekers a transformative event and cultivates face to face encounters with the most vulnerable. Since her retirement from her youth ministry, she continues to gather and distribute donations of food, warmth, comforting beanie babies, and gift cards to the unhoused on the Albuquerque streets, listening to their stories and offering dignity. She remains particularly mindful of the youth and women with children.

A Boy Named Bishop

Fittingly, it seems.
Named as a blessing.
Saving innumerable lives
at the age of ten.
What wonders, with
the rest of your life?!
Reimagining my own
ten-year-old self . . .
deep in play
and in imagination.

Are the children
wired differently now,
to have such profound caring?
Such deep knowing of
the bigger world?
His father speaks of
our internal genius,
and clearly nurtures his son's.
With the aid of 3-D printing,
a device to prevent
hot car infant deaths.
But it is that caring.
That awareness and love
for others' well-being,
that sticks, after all.

Bishop Curry—his story

As a ten-year-old boy in Texas, he was heartbroken to learn of a baby in his neighborhood who died in an overheated minivan. He had previously designed his own catapult and ping pong ball cannon and decided to come up with a device to prevent further infant deaths. He made a few drawings and then showed them to his father, who works in process engineering at Toyota. The device would attach to a car seat and would detect when the car has come to a stop and if there's a child in the car seat. "If the temperature begins to heat up, the device then begins to blow cold air on the baby while at the same time sending a message to the parents or caregivers." "If they don't respond, then the device would alert authorities and paramedics."

Bishop named his invention "Oasis" and he and his dad built a 3D model. They then decided they needed to patent the device and create a real prototype. But they soon learned that intellectual property lawyers charge high fees. When someone suggested they try crowdsourcing money, the Currys didn't expect their invention would get much attention. Instead, they managed to raise more than US $29,000 on GoFundMe in less than six months.

The family has now been able to submit invention patent documentation to the U.S. Patent and Trademark Office and are waiting to hear back from them before beginning the manufacturing process.

Protest Unsuccessful

Sometimes it just takes more
to execute change.
Sometimes
another forty years
and no doubt
lives in that bargain.
Reading of
such a passionate stance.
Fierce refusal of any more abuse.
Crushing to know that it
still was not enough.

Did the daily torture
then just resume,
once the noise died down?
Did they all just go back to work?
Did the audience grow at all?
Or did everyone just look away again?
Carmelita Torres was only seventeen,
when she showed up on the
Santa Fe bridge as the warrior heroine.
Basta!
was the cry of the day,
prompting thousands to join in.

And then the men, too.

Carmelita Torres—her story

In the early nineteen-hundreds on the Texas/Mexican border, it was standard procedure to daily 'disinfect' the hundreds of day laborers commuting across the bridges from Juarez to El Paso. This included stripping naked and being doused with an assortment of toxins, including gasoline, kerosene, sulfuric acid, and Zyklon B, a cyanide-based pesticide, which was later used in the gas chambers of Nazi Germany. As a part of the de-lousing process, strip searches were conducted, along with reported photographing of the women. At the culmination of the resulting riot, several women including Carmelita Torres were arrested.

But then the Immigration Act of 1917 was passed just days later, imposing further barriers for Mexican laborers entering the U.S., including literacy tests and taxes. Despite the disruption of the riots, the status quo of disinfecting would continue for another forty years, leaving one to wonder what became of that courageous seventeen-year-old.

Leader of the Night Witches

Bold, determined, and ultimately successful
in over twenty-four thousand missions.
The Order of Suvarov was hers alone,
as a woman pilot.
Twenty-three of her regiment
also recognized for their courage.
Obsolete Polikapov biplanes
of mostly canvas and plywood,
too light for equipment like a parachute,
without sophisticated radar,
but festooned bravely with flowers.

Only two bombs at a time
requiring multiple sorties every night.
Engines idling, they glided over their targets
in those hand-me-down uniforms,
and oversize boots, freezing in open cockpits.
After releasing their projectiles,
an expedition onto the wing
required to restart the engine.
Fierceness and accuracy
earned the German epithet, Night Witches,
taken as a badge of honor,
proud of their acumen
in those modified crop dusters.
Perhaps if more opportunities
were afforded to women . . .

Yevdokiya Bershanskaya—her story

Yevdokiya Bershankaya was regimental commander of the Russian 46th Taman Guards Night Bomber Aviation Regiment during World War II. The Soviets were the first to allow women to fly combat missions. Her regiment of all women pilots, aged seventeen to twenty-six, was known collectively for its heroic feats for the USSR, in over 23,000 sorties, and was referred to by the Germans as the Night Witches, due to their strategy of stalling their Polikarpov Po-2 open-cockpit biplanes to glide in over German targets, with only a soft whooshing sound. The insubstantial planes were ill-equipped, outdated, and too noisy for any kind of stealth approach, thus the dangerous stall. They were shot at relentlessly, often flying through a wall of enemy fire, and with planes left peppered with bullet holes. Since the lightweight planes could only carry two bombs at a time, pilots often flew eight or more missions a night. Feared and even loathed, an Iron Cross was awarded automatically to any German pilot who downed a Night Witch.

In Terms of Hectares

A legion of eco warriors
some as a solo initiative
each in a different country

Laboring for this shared planet
so much in need
some of them for decades

Hikmet Kaya began his mission
as a forest management chief
in northern Turkey

Nearly a half century later
there are birds, butterflies,
mammals and reptiles
on that formerly arid wasteland

He brought his skills
to those thirty million saplings

His pantheon of cohorts
in India, Indonesia, and Brazil
offer similar successes

Lush forests returning balance
replacing what was barren
with fruit-laden trees
and flowing water
replenishing the lungs of our planet

Hikmet Kaya—his story

The eco warriors are as young as ten years old. The one in India began when she was four. A movement happening simultaneously in numerous countries, one of its most obvious heroes is Hikmet Kaya, a retired forest management chief in northern Turkey who has totally transformed a massive, barren stepped land beginning during his tenure as chief in 1978 and continuing for the following forty-one years. His reforestation project near the city of Sinop has created a lush landscape, thirty million trees richer, with habitat for a vast number of returning species of insects, butterflies, mammals, and reptiles.

Similar projects are underway in Ghana, China, India, Indonesia, and Brazil. The Philippines has passed a law requiring students to plant ten trees prior to graduation. Pakistan conceived a project to plant ten billion trees on desert land, employing 63,000 laborers, thus helping to alleviate a bit of the unemployment crisis there. In Ethiopia, students, government officials, and assorted environmentalists joined at over a thousand sites, planting more than 350 million saplings in just twelve hours.

> *"Just as a 4 mm seed grows into a 100 feet tall tree, I know that I should never underestimate my power even if I am just a child. I can make a significant contribution in creating an impact."* —Prasiddhi Singh

I've read that planting just seven trees will replace the oxygen used in your entire life. Let's do it, in case it's true. *pjww*

Untold Immortality

Henrietta's life seemingly common
for her time.
Mother of five children.
Sudden cancer diagnosis at Johns Hopkins.
Her only option in 1951
a segregated ward.
Standard practice
to take a sample of that tumor.
The word consent never considered.
Irony that her boundless gift would
have brought her such wondrous joy.
Those cells shared freely by the
hospital, doubling daily in number,
unlike any other cells.
Her later generations question ethics
while searching for any respect.

All these years later, she has become
known for her impact in changing
modern medicine. Her cells crucial
to developing a vast array of vaccines.
Polio.   HIV.   And Covid.
Her impact unfathomably broad.
Cancer and in-vitro research.
Her genome sequenced.
Her life now celebrated in scholarships
and annual lectures hosting a thousand.
Despite her passing at age thirty-one,
her cells are alive over seventy years hence.

Henrietta Lacks—her story

Her death at an early age from cervical cancer held so much significance for the advancement of modern medicine that her simple life paled in comparison. From that moment forward, her rare, rapidly reproducing cancer cells were distributed freely by Johns Hopkins Hospital for research. In 1951, no consent was required, either by the patient or their family. Henrietta's five children struggled to survive beyond her passing, with her disabled daughter passing as well at fifteen years old. It was several decades after Henrietta's death that her children were asked if they were related to the famed HeLa cells, by then widely known for their impact in research and virus immunization. Her children had begun receiving calls requesting blood samples and their medical histories had been published in journals without their permission. Respect was not involved, and Henrietta's descendants lost billions of dollars that they were entitled to as her cells were distributed more and more widely across the globe. More recently her contribution was recognized and celebrated in huge annual events and through medical scholarships honoring her gift to us all. But it took over seventy years for the first lawsuit to reach a settlement, with the Lacks family carefully avoiding culpability for any university or teaching hospital using the cells for research. Henrietta's legacy truly is immortal.

Las Libras

Veronica Cruz began by freeing
those first nine women,
wrongly charged with infanticide.
A miscarriage could qualify.
In a centuries-old global tradition of
women helping other women,
she built a network rich in creativity.
Pills sequestered under the batting
in a box of souvenir earrings
—para las chicas.
Or perhaps in a packet of seeds.
Concern for what may happen
on either side of that imaginary line.
Trusting that enforcement
of expatriates is complex.

The acompanantes
with their surplus to be shared.
New designations created
for these fearful and disruptive times,
as fourteen states lost their collective minds
and proceeded to ruin lives.
Pondering how to connect with
this saint of the needy,
vowing that there must be a way
to qualify as one of the old hippies,
even on this side. The risk?
removal of reproductive rights.
The irony not lost that big pharma
could inadvertently be heroic, too.

Veronica Cruz—her story

The post-Roe abortion underground hasn't taken long to develop. Heroes on both sides of the Mexican/U.S. border have banded together to protect the lives of the women in states where abortion is no longer a safe and available option. In Texas, for example, turning someone in for aiding in providing abortion pills could be worth $10,000., as some laws revert to nineteenth century mindsets. In contrast, activists like Veronica Cruz have so successfully reduced the stigma of abortion that the Supreme Court of Mexico decriminalized it in 2021. The abortion-inducing pills, widely available in Mexico have helped over two thousand women have abortions, despite heavy fines and threat of jail time in some states. Connecting the dots, Cruz connects supplies from Mexico with willing distributors in the U.S. who then mail pills to those in need.

Having grown up on a farm, in a time when abortion was taboo, she has witnessed the trajectory of how public health is impacted disproportionately for the poor. In 2000, Mexico had legislated abortion as illegal even for rape victims, prompting Cruz to start Las Libras, a nonprofit offering the sharing of pills and experiences of those who already had abortions—thus reducing the fear and stigma. The acompanantes. Having assembled a team of lawyers, Cruz sought out women wrongly held for abortion-related crimes in Mexico (despite circumstances such as miscarriage) and secured their release. In Cruz's view, women have a moral duty to support one another when the state fails to guarantee their rights.

For Some, a Choice

For Rick Rescorla, his origins in a tiny village in
Cornwall seemed an unlikely beginning.
The trajectory of our lives so often mysterious.
Enlisting in both Cyprus and Rhodesia
stoked his fierce stance for justice.
Then lured by the next opportunity in Viet Nam,
the array of medals belied his ongoing smile.
He stood for morality and personified respect,
dismissing that film glorifying his bravery,
citing heroes as those who died.

After the war, as head of security for Dean Witter,
his mettle as a strategist proved itself
again and again.
Observations of structural vulnerability
as the tallest target.
Drills in the stairwells of the towers.
Who else could have imagined?
The truck bombing made his speculations
seem uncanny, with the perpetrators as predicted.
Then as the unfathomable horror he had warned of
unfurled, he guided all the company employees
down those stairs, despite directives to the contrary.
Returning repeatedly, he insisted on
certainty of everyone's safety.
Over twenty-seven hundred people
were saved in following Rick's Cornish songs
down those stairs.

Rick's new wife understood just a bit of who he was,
aside from the man who loved to dance with her
or sit in quiet meditation.
She had seen those medals
he chose to put away.
His triumph over cancer only hinted at his strength.
She had first encountered him running barefoot.
And ultimately, she grew to know him and his honor
ever more deeply after he was gone.

Rick Rescorla—his story

Some are just innately drawn to a cause, to fighting communism or some other injustice. Rick was destined to be such a warrior, always with a smile on his face. Recipient of assorted medals for bravery from three conflicts, he subsequently headed up security for Dean Witter, headquartered in the World Trade Center. Ironically, he had recommended the company's move to New Jersey, where there was far less threat of any kind. But the lease extended for another five years. Meanwhile, he had accurately predicted the truck bombing, pinpointing the likely instigators.

He routinely insisted that the employees all participate in evacuation drills, marching down the stairwell in pairs from the forty-fourth floor. Also in the meantime, he had met the great love of his life in his fifties and was enjoying shared travels, dancing whenever possible, and leading a more meditative existence than in much of his life previously. But he remained a hero at heart. And his beloved was required to find peace in knowing that he could not have lived on, any other way than as such a hero to so many.

Misplaced Apostle to the Apostles

Inspired by Cynthia Bourgault

Her own gospel was there.
Deleted in that patriarchal way,
leaving a repressed and gravely wounded
divine feminine, communion denied.
We watch the repeated dynamic
pervasively played out in boundless examples
from sexual harassment in a Minnesota iron mine
to degradation in a supreme court hearing.
Sixteen hundred years to refine and deepen
that dysfunctional comfort zone.
From its inception,
fluid and diverse.
Prayers for its resurrection.

Where have you been for so long,
voice silenced,
while we careened through
assorted shadow interpretations
in the darkness?
Celebration now, for glimmers
of the transformative alchemy
of kenotic love,
with all its glorious interwoven archetypes.
Beloved.

Mary Magdalene—her story

One of the most controversial and misunderstood figures of Christianity, Mary Magdalene was the sole feminine gospel author as well as the sole woman apostle. Always present and always first, (i.e. after the resurrection), her teachings on our purpose to be fully human, with a limitless soul and embodying transformative love offered a major influence in the history of Christianity. Mary was perceived to have the best understanding of Jesus's teachings. Though commonly thought a prostitute even today, there was no biblical reference to this effect. Jesus was said to have 'cured' her of seven demons.

Her story sparks curiosity, controversy, and veneration, with all copies of her gospel ordered destroyed in the fourth century. Buried in the desert by monks in Egypt, her teachings survived in part, offering a glimpse into a kind of Christianity lost for nearly fifteen hundred years . . . it presents a radical interpretation of Jesus' teachings as a path to inner spiritual knowledge, rejecting His death as the path to eternal life. It presents the most clear, convincing argument in any early Christian writing for the legitimacy of women's leadership with a sharp critique of illegitimate power and a utopian vision of spiritual perfection; it challenges our romantic views about the harmony and unanimity of the first Christians; and it asks us to rethink the basis for church authority. Mary truly represented early feminists.

Gabions Effecting Eco-Diversity

Beginning with *trincheras*
minus the cattle
and the grasses reemerge.
Followed by the forerunner avian life.
Over half the US species were here
and they are returning.
A socialite from the upper east side
made the best story
while Josiah built the first *trinchera*.
Conversion via the Yaqui minnow,
from New Yorkers oblivious to weather.

Four ranches draped across our southern border
now host exploding diversity
in this crucible for revival.
Valer envisions a new swimming hole
for the bears and someday
the return of the beavers.
The mantra: slow the water.
Researchers come now and a foundation
pays young Mexicans to remain and restore.
Neighboring ranchers turn naturalists.
And in her spare time
Valer taught herself Spanish.

Valer and Josiah Austin—their story

Purchased on a lark, they said, but with that drive to do something meaningful, these New Yorkers ended up with multiple ranches totaling tens of thousands of acres of parched desert, mostly dry for over 150 years, straddling the Mexican border. This land is a part of the Madrean Archipelago, historically one of the most bio-diverse areas on the planet. Over half the bird species in the US, over 3,000 plant species (some exclusively), and a lengthy list of rare and endangered mammals have called this land home. As many as 500 species of bees, the highest concentration on earth, come from here. After the cattle were relocated, a simple tradition of boulder dams to slow the monsoon rains illustrated how to restore the land to its former rich diversity, a work in progress with astonishing success. The native trees and grasses lost to the mining industry have reappeared and the marshland is again thriving. Neighboring ranchers now thrill to the jaguars gracing their property and the river flowing.

With some irony, the Austins' restoration efforts have greater potential to stem the flow of drugs or people than Trump's wall, with people crossing on foot having a much harder time coming upriver now. Those dry washes used to be the highway for coming across. The Austins' foundation, *Cuenca los Ojos*, https://www.cuencalosojos.org/, promoting holistic land management and water conservation, has the following stated mission: "To protect, restore, and rewild the biodiversity of the U.S.-Mexico Borderlands. We bring back Water, Soil, and Life." And they have.

Her Name was Sybil Ludington

New heroines so often emerging
into the light, in this time.
Malala, Greta Thunberg,
our own Ariana Saludares.
And then, so many not celebrated in their own day.
Whether in some scientific disclosure,
deep in algorithms and formulas unfathomable,
or simply a young girl in a dress,
courageous teen-aged patriot
spreading alarm for impending British attack.

Unrecognized, still, in any history book.
Yet high on my own list of hopeful heroes.
Eldest of twelve. She was no doubt
accustomed to taking charge.
How many of us can imagine that ride?
Forty miles in the night. Rough and
unlit country backroads. Driving rain
in her face as she stood in her stirrups.
Unlike Paul Revere, she evaded capture.
Qualified, today, as badass.
Standing proudly alongside
Emma Gonzalez.
#emmaforchange.

Sybil Ludington—her story

All these years later, a bronze statue commemorates her courage, and a postage stamp honored her for our national Bicentennial. Child of a militia Colonel commanding four hundred men, Sybil Ludington was raised a patriot with leadership in her genes. She learned of British plans to attack the Danbury, Connecticut stockpile of provisions and arms through her father's network. At the time, her father's regiment was disbanded for the requirements of planting season, miles apart, each working their farms. The rider who had brought the alarm was too exhausted to continue and her father was preparing for the battle. So, at age sixteen, mounting her horse, Star, encouraging him with a stick, Sybil rode all night through a driving rainstorm, all on the rugged country roads of Putnam County, New York, to warn of the upcoming attack. Alerted by her warning and responding to her urging, hundreds of Patriots met the British troops at Ridgefield, Connecticut and successfully repelled them to Long Island Sound.

She subsequently married and had one son. Her husband served in the military as her father had. A savvy businesswoman, Sybil bought a tavern, selling it for three times what she had paid. After her son's death she applied for a military pension, which was denied, based on insufficient proof of marriage, resulting in her dying in poverty. One can now follow historical markers, tracking her Putnam County ride, to honor her.

No Skills Required

A Doctor, in fact. Inspired by LeBron,
she rollerbladed into the World Trade Center
to give aid to survivors.
This is the look of a
full-time humanitarian.
Child of Aussie missionaries,
told of being at home in chaos.
She is described as sharing light.
She's the one who recruited Sean Penn
to come to Haiti and partner the work,
bringing all those rental party tents
and giving the storm victims
food and shelter while FEMA dithered.

Now in Ukraine, where
civilians become soldiers,
the world has her back.
She is magnetically
drawn to dire situations.
Torniquets bringing tears,
she is training warriors in CPR.
Collaborations inevitably result.
Her bottom line: "We won't
let this terror overtake us."

Alison Thompson—her story

Born to Aussie missionary parents, her heart leads Dr. Alison Thompson to where there is need. The world's introduction to her was in Sri Lanka, where she developed the 'Third Wave Volunteers' with an accompanying tsunami warning system, book, and documentary. She later appeared in Haiti as the doer she is, making things happen and saving lives. She has shown up at various catastrophes worldwide, pitching in to evacuate orphans or simply to be sure that people are fed. Now working in Ukraine, she says, "If you are inclined to pitch in, please come. If nothing else, your loving presence, hugging people is needed. Medical expertise is always welcomed, too." Teaching civilians cum military commanders simple first aid can bring them to tears. While everyone is there to offer aid, it is the women who find the most open doors in this devastated country. The caretakers. Just sending foot powder or a helmet to the fisherman in combat is valuable. Feeding people, housing people, saving lives. And in the end, Alison Thompson is certain that love wins.

The Steps of Progress

Changing the narrative in just one generation.
Rejection of the unequal on a southern plantation.

No to slavery.

No to subordinate women.

Education for all.

Introduction to justice by Quaker beliefs,
Tolerance and truth for all.
Radicalized in stages,
finally seeking direct action
beyond the peaceful Friends.
Publishing their passions
as abolitionists and suffragettes
ultimately rendered them outsiders to many.
The first of their gender to
so publicly demand
equal rights for women.
Despite their eloquent vocalizations,
finally deemed more effective
from a distance,
they founded schools
and raised their brother's biracial offspring,
continuing to raise their voices.

The Grimké Sisters—their story

Two early and prominent activists for abolition and women's rights, Sarah Grimké and Angelina Grimké Weld grew up in the cradle of slavery on a South Carolina plantation. Their father owned many slaves, with both parents believing women subordinate to men. Through their own studies, the sisters concluded that women should have equal rights, with slavery abolished. Angelina was particularly outspoken. In her twenties, Sarah spent time in Philadelphia with the Quakers, tolerant of both causes. She moved there, converting to Quakerism, with Angelina following. Here, they both published abolitionist writings to great praise. They wanted to advance both causes, but many abolitionists were uncomfortable with women having equality. Likewise, many women's rights advocates were against abolishing slavery. This made them outsiders in both communities. They traveled giving talks on both causes. Their views on slavery were highly respected since they had grown up in a slave-holding family and understood the system more intimately than Northern abolitionists. Angelina, considered one of the most powerful speakers in the movement, was the first American woman to address a legislative body when she spoke on abolition and women's rights before the Massachusetts legislature.

But as their fame spread, a backlash against them grew. Many were unhappy to see women taking a public role in social and political debates, especially angry that they spoke to audiences of both genders and races. Angelina spoke to the 4-day abolitionist convention with a noisy protest mob gathered outside. After the rest of the convention was canceled to restore peace, the mob broke into the empty building and set fire to it, with the structure being allowed to burn to the ground. Sarah and Angelina continued to write and support the abolitionist cause, though never taking a prominent role in the movement again, subsequently opening schools. Upon learning that their brother had fathered three children with his slave, they welcomed the children into their family, paying for their education. The two eldest nephews became civil rights activists.

"All I ask of our brethren is that they take their feet off our necks."

—Ruth Bader Ginsburg

arguing before the U.S. Supreme Court,

quoting abolitionist Sarah Grimké.

Invitation

But, wait, I said. I wasn't invited.
Of course you are, Park the car, he insisted,
in what I came to recognize as
his signature style.
Always included and always expected
to join in the celebration and the service
whether a simple well-executed meal
with friends
or tutoring in planting in Palomas.
A brilliant silversmith in his past life,
ultimately training those in his homeland
to facilitate the work
inspiring and energizing as he went.
Excelling in each new capacity,
transferable skills from metal to wood,
From small business development
to organic heirloom apples.
Mentoring in each new incarnation.
A legacy of such an array of passions
and boundless solidarity.

Juan Velasco—his story

Bolivian born, Juan came to the U.S. at eighteen for college and graduate school, then beginning a diverse trajectory from managing a spice company, working as a wall street banker, nurturing an heirloom apple orchard, passionately defending the environment in everything he did and taught, always supporting young leadership however he could. A mentor to most all in his orbit, he was a founding member of the New Mexico Men's Wellness group in 1985, one of the first such men's groups in the country. Support for other writers, artists and businessmen was a natural offshoot. He spent time in Santa Fe with his own jewelry business, training apprentices in Bolivia to do his craft. He and his wife, Suzanne, started a nonprofit providing university scholarships and supporting community-based projects, called con Bolivia, In Puerto Palomas, Mexico, working with Border Partners offered more rich opportunities for his teaching small business development and mentoring in all of his skills. His fearless opinions were matched by his fearless generosity and never failed to inspire others to step up.

"We make a living by what we get but we make a life by what we give."
—Juan Velasco

Minty, No More

Identity, attached to place.
Or for some, the primacy
of one's very being.
Altogether separate
from location, culture.
Watching the replication
of Harriet's run for her life,
the hounds in her ear,
but hearing the louder voice of God.
And then the expansion,
the empowerment,
as her beliefs manifested.
All her people, deserving.
She never lost a. single. soul.
Again, the question rises,
where does our own courage lie?
Thinking, in these times
of just such disparity,
It may well be tested.

Later, as emboldened and armed
scout and spy for the Union army,
the first woman to lead,
and one of those elite cadres
of women warriors through history.
Strategist and recruiter,
she collaborated with
the storied John Brown.

By the time of Combahee,
the volume of those liberated
surpassed seven hundred at once,
under her command of over
three hundred former slaves,
the 54th Massachusetts Infantry Regiment.

Harriet Tubman—her story

Born Araminta Ross, Harriet was nearly killed as a child by a blow to the head from a lead weight hurled by an angry overseer trying to get her to help tie another slave. She suffered from relentless head pain and debilitating seizures for the rest of her life. Despite this, she worked the timber fields with her father and brothers, learning invaluable skills as a naturalist for her future work in guiding people to safety—what plants were edible or medicinal, astronomy, tides, weather, trapping, and understanding wildlife.

In the 19th century, the famed Mason-Dixon line that formed the Pennsylvania-Maryland border was viewed as the invisible demarcation between freedom and slavery. Her return over that line more than thirteen times to rescue her family members and others constituted the ultimate in risk. After the passage of the Fugitive Slave Act, Philadelphia was no longer the safe haven of her arrival, so Tubman moved on to New York and Canada with her work in the Underground Railroad. She spent much of the balance of her life working for civil rights, women's rights, and lecturing for justice. During the Civil War, she worked as a scout, spy, and nurse for the US Army, the first American woman to lead an armed raid. She opened the first nursing homes for Blacks, cementing her steadfast conviction of health care as a universal human right.

from Robert Hayden, U.S. Poet Laureate, honoring Harriet Tubman:

Hoot-owl calling in the ghosted air,

Five times calling to the hants in the air,

Shadow of a face in the scary leaves,

Shadow of a voice in the talking leaves.

Just a Simple Secretary

She always remained faithful to her humanity,
saying it was the right thing to do.
Repeated risk in taking food, supplies, and news
to those she sheltered.
Over two years as protector, guardian.
A fierce advocate even after they were revealed.

Examining now the degree of my own valor,
I ponder how to bring a frightened family home.
To give them sanctuary.
Share what I have,
most of all my hope.
Hmm, could we revive
the underground railroad?
Reminded of that tunnel at the Buckhorn.
Leading to the old fort, we were told.

Miep's taciturn husband said only
that one night he might not return.
Her own last bold foray in courage was
to gather the writing, all those
hundreds of loose pages,
becoming an ambassador for the words
and the truth told by a young girl.
She, herself, humbly claimed only to
stand at the end of a long line of heroes.
Carrying the burden of sadness,
that she was unable to save them all.

Miep Gies—her story

Born in Vienna during World War I, in a time of food scarcity, Miep was often ill as a child. A Dutch family offered care and healing, giving her family hope for a safer life for her. In her twenties she began working for Otto Frank, a Jewish man who had moved to Holland with his wife and two daughters, Margot and Anne, also in search of safety. Jews were being increasingly persecuted, and the Franks finally found it necessary to all stay in secret upper, rear rooms in Otto's office building. This secret annex was accessed by a revolving bookcase.

For over two years, Miep, the loyal secretary, procured food and supplies for the eight people hidden over the warehouse. They were required to be absolutely silent during the hours of business, for fear of discovery. Miep went out several times a day to differing sources to purchase food so that she was never seen carrying too much at one time. Bags were often hidden under her coat. She did not share her secret even with her family, for their safety. When the officers finally did find the annex, Miep was spared arrest because the commanding officer was from her community in Vienna. Despite her gathering funds in an attempt to secure release for her friends, she was unsuccessful and ultimately, only Otto survived the concentration camps. Miep did rescue Anne's diaries and returned them to Otto after the end of the war. She later insisted that she only did her duty as a human being, helping friends in need.

No Handicap

Not hindered for even a moment
by that ill-fitted prosthetic leg,
Virginia Hall took on the Nazis
behind the lines,
wreaking havoc beyond imagination.
No one could conceive of
her accomplishments,
often disguised as
someone equally unlikely.

Nicknames included the
Witch and the Madonna,
depending on perspective.
Her fervor for her beloved France
carried her to
becoming the sole operative
to change the course of the war—
and often in an unsanctioned way.

Such a vivid example
of what can be done outside of
the constraints of rule and assignment.
Surreptitiously darting
from one hidden lair to the next,
while lugging an unwieldy radio,
she managed both sabotage
and supply drops,
supported by a cadre of loyal believers.
Her pain lay in the knowledge that whoever
was detained in her stead was tortured mercilessly.
But the Resistance triumphed in the end.

Virginia Hall—her story

An American spy during World War II, former Baltimore socialite, and the first Allied woman behind enemy lines, she was credited with changing the course of the war. In her thirties, with an endlessly painful prosthetic leg from a hunting accident, she began her military duty in a medical capacity. Ultimately, she helped to pioneer the daredevil role of espionage, subversion, and sabotage in enemy territory, in an era when women were largely ignored, their contributions mostly supportive and palliative. To even her closest confidants during the war, she seemed to be without family or assigned regiment, with only a burning determination to defeat the Nazis. She was, for a time, considered their most dangerous adversary. Having always defied convention and embraced adversity, she had excelled at languages, weaving her way through prohibition, segregation and the lure of such changing times. She spent time in France, adopting it as her second country and subsequently worked with the French resistance fighting fascism.

She posed as a reporter for the *Washington Post*, actually sending them stories as her cover, while developing elaborate disguises to aid in her daringly smuggling messages under the Nazis' noses and radioing locations for food and supply drops. She trained other subversives in explosives and sabotage, disrupting the Nazi supply lines, as well as leading ambushes of incoming supplies of fuel and food for the Nazis. Referred to as the Madonna by those who respected her, she commanded her own guerrilla force for a time and was ultimately the only civilian woman in WW II to be awarded the distinguished service cross.

Diné Victory at Iwo Jima

Originally twenty-nine warriors.
Finally, over five hundred engaged
in the battle for their land.
Their.   Land.
Unwritten words, unpronounceable
to others. With further encryption,
impenetrable.
Ironically taboo in Indian schools
back home at that time.
And further irony
in that land taken from them.
A different brand of patriotism
than what we can fathom.
Credit for Iwo Jima's victory.

And then back at home . . .
with ongoing disrespect,
we call it Monument Valley.
Sadly, I don't know its proper name,
something with great reverence
I'm certain.
And not John Ford Point.
Stewart always insisted on
Kasha-Katuwe
rather than Tent Rocks.
The least we can offer.
And don't even let me begin
to speak of Mt. Rushmore.

Navajo Code Talkers—their story

Chester Nez was said to be the last of these courageous warriors, (of the "*Diné* " people in their language), alive until 2014. He had been recruited by the U.S. Marines from his 'Indian School' in Arizona in 1942. The intention of these schools was to strip the youth of their heritage and their spirit, as well as their native languages, a cruel paradox. After recruitment, there was skepticism that the youth could qualify . . .

Ultimately the military leaders conceded that the native language was impenetrable, despite there being no words for contemporary military equipment. With substituted terms like big fish for battleship, strategies were safeguarded from the Japanese. The Navajo code talkers took part in every assault the U.S. Marines conducted in the Pacific from 1942 to 1945. They served in all six Marine divisions, Marine Raider battalions, and Marine parachute units, transmitting messages by phone and radio in their native language, a code that the Japanese never broke. In the first two days of the battle at Iwo Jima, 800 messages were transmitted without error. The Code Talkers, who had brought their culture along as equipment, received medals after the war, if no more respect. Within their communities, healing ceremonies offered them reintegration back home. But finally in 2022, descendants of these men broke sacred ground in northern New Mexico for a dedicated Navajo Code Talkers Museum. There are multiple exhibits in other NM and AZ museums, as well.

During The Fall

The Midway was the Major's first sight of any aircraft carrier,
noted at one point to have twenty-six Hueys circling.
Having hot-wired his family's escape, his base under fire,
as the last Marine guards fled the roof of the embassy,
joining the aerial traffic.

Aiming for open sea.   Trusting.
The Bird Dog an unlikely vehicle with little fuel, no radio,
fixed landing gear, designed for reconnaissance.
Falling in with a convoy of copters
leaving the coast for freedom.

'Wife and five child aboard,' he wrote,
insisting on space to land on that carrier.
The bold captain did clear that deck,
of an untold number of choppers sacrificed for a family
now U.S. Citizens
And that Bird Dog proudly displayed in our aviation museum.

Oh, and the crew on the *Midway*
took up a collection for the family.

Major Buang-Ly—his story

April, 1975

As South Vietnam was collapsing under an onslaught of communist forces, with their leader having resigned, and panic abounding, Saigon was surrounded by communist troops. An American radio station began playing "White Christmas," the signal for any remaining evacuees to go to their evacuation points. South Vietnamese Air Force pilot, Major Buang-Ly was among few remaining on Tan Son Nhut Air Base, where many aircraft had been destroyed by shelling. Carrying as many possessions as possible, Buang-Ly spotted a two-seater Cessna O-1 Bird Dog on the airfield. He crammed his wife, five small children, and belongings into the Cessna, hotwired the small craft, and took off over open water.

Thirty minutes out to sea, he spotted helicopters ahead and thought they surely had a landing target. Upon approaching the *Midway*, he was compromised without radio or flotation devices and running out of fuel. He began circling, rocking his wings, and dropping notes, which blew off the carrier deck. Finally, a third note tucked in the holster of his sidearm landed: "Can you mouve [sic] these Helicopter to the other side, I can land on your runway, I can fly 1 hour more, we have enough time to mouve. Please rescue me, Major Buang wife and 5 child." Navy Captain Lawrence Chambers, new at command of the *Midway*, was instructed by his admiral to let the plane ditch and then rescue them by chopper. Chambers knew the plane would flip with its fixed landing gear, making survival impossible, so he began to have the deck cleared. Imagining court martial, he deliberately did not keep count of how many helicopters were pushed off the deck to make room for what turned out to be a perfect landing by the man who had never seen an aircraft carrier.

Today, Major Buang is ninety-four and living in Florida with his family all citizens. The Bird Dog is proudly displayed in our national aviation museum in Pensacola, Florida.

The Meaning of Death

He painted a target on his own back
aware of the growing anger against him.
Knew his time was short
and meant to make it count.
Knight of Swords in a time of change and chaos.
Harvey listened. Made a safe haven in his shop
for all the disenfranchised and rejected.
Ran and ran again. A megaphone on the
street corner, looking everyone in the eye.

Finally, the city listened, too,
a historic moment for the country.
Relentless in putting a human face
on politics, he defended rights, successfully.
Only a few short weeks later,
the culmination of the hate.
Despite his stand against violence,
Harvey followed George in death.
Tens of thousands showed up in honor,
candles in hand, his hope in their hearts.
That bullet blew the door wide open.

Harvey Milk—his story

Harvey Milk, a visionary civil and human rights leader was one of the first openly gay elected officials in the United States winning a seat on the San Francisco Board of Supervisors in 1977. Milk's unprecedented loud and unapologetic proclamation of his authenticity as an openly gay candidate for public office, and his subsequent election gave never before experienced hope to LGBT people everywhere, at a time when the community was encountering widespread hostility and discrimination. His remarkable career was tragically cut short when he was assassinated nearly a year after taking office. Following a stint in the Navy, Milk entered the civilian working world in New York, as a teacher, a stock analyst, and a production associate for Broadway musicals. During the 1960s and early 70s, he became more actively involved in politics and advocacy and demonstrated against the Vietnam War.

Late 1972, Milk moved to San Francisco, opening a camera store on Castro Street, in the heart of the city's growing gay community. It quickly became a neighborhood center. Milk's sense of humor and theatricality made him a popular figure. Little more than a year after his arrival in the city, he declared his candidacy for the San Francisco Board of Supervisors. He lost twice but emerged as a force to be reckoned with in local politics. Milk and a few other business owners founded the Castro Village Association, a first in the nation organizing of predominantly LGBT businesses, with Milk as president. He organized the Castro Street Fair in 1974 to attract more customers to area businesses. Its success made the Castro Village Association an effective power base for gay merchants and a blueprint for other LGBT communities in the US, with Harvey as a powerful advocate for strong, safe neighborhoods. Harvey was included in Time magazine's list of the "100 most important people of the 20th century and posthumously received the Medal of Freedom from President Barack Obama, who praised Milk's "visionary courage and conviction" in fighting discrimination.

Pop Culture Fueling the Greater Good

Offering tools to outliers for their future.
Surmounting disconnect by
marrying fun and work
while overcoming boredom.
Influencing outcome
by critical training.
Displaying evolution in action.
Harnessing resources for the greater good.
Laparoscopic testament of the possible.
Aviation parallels abounding as evidence.
Capitalizing on competitive natures
to advance skills.

Training afield in Aruba to launch and inspire.
Working to restore the nation's winning streak.
Working toward mastery
on a moment-to-moment basis.
Driving diversity and its perspectives.
Collaborative competition
climbing over malaise,
jump-starting momentum,
transforming systems.

Games for good.

James ‘Butch’ Rosser Jr.—his story

Coming from a legacy of firsts and a belief in something bigger, Rosser is breaking barriers. A surgeon, a scientist, and a parent, Butch Rosser is shining a light on the deficiencies of our education system, illustrating new possibilities for inclusion, innovation, and progress into a new age of teaching and training. Tying the skills required for manning a video console to the parallel dexterity of laparoscopic surgery, Rosser has introduced a new world of possibilities for many marginalized youth in this country, through presentations in schools, as well as offering training to those already in the medical field, revolutionizing what can be done, surgically, with fewer errors and at what greatly reduced times. Statistics prove much improved skills, showing evolution in action, both in developing children and in those already in the medical field. Studies have shown that games can even help in diagnosing depression. Rosser promotes collaborative competition, allowing for knowledge transfer strategies and cutting-edge change in teaching and education—long overdue. He touts a visionary shift in how video games can be viewed as a vehicle for the launch into the digital age of surgery, a remarkable trajectory from the inception of Pong in 1972.

Aviation demonstrates this same type of remote ability in instrument flying. Building and flying miniature drone planes is Dr. Rosser’s leisure pastime, while developing drone certification programs for students to explore what careers await them in drone mastery.

From a Kernel of Inclusion

Janice and Cecil's vision ever-expanding.
Today, over six decades later,
a growing institution thrives
in the Tenderloin,
the tenacious beating heart
of the City,
serving the community
and well beyond.
There's a mobile recovery unit,
or you could become a justice warrior
or help to surmount food insecurity.

Marvin, the poet preacher
offers notebooks and pencils
for the writers' church.
But you need to stop to
absorb the splendor of the orchestra.
A saxophone. And drums.
And the glorious horns.
And the potency of the Ensemble,
voices raised in sublime joy.
Proof that inclusivity reigns.

Over forty years ago, I took my
visiting mother there, where she was
startled and pleased to be invited
to hug everyone within reach.

Rev. Cecil Williams and Janice Mirikitani—their story

In 1963, when Cecil Williams became minister, Glide Memorial Church in San Francisco had a congregation just barely in double digits. Thanks to the stewardship of this fierce duo over six decades, Glide's social services (free meals, housing support, and recovery programs) serve tens of thousands annually, meaning its "community" extends far beyond formal church membership. Glide's Free Meals Program, launched in 1980, provides three free hot meals a day to anyone in need, dishing out hundreds of thousands of meals each year. After SNAP benefits were cut in the fall of 2025, one day's lunch count was over a thousand people. Today, Glide is the City's largest provider of social services, with Williams referred to as the conscience of San Francisco. Based on inclusivity and love, with a welcoming approach to the LGBT community and unflinching support of civil rights, Cecil and Janice built this church into the institution it is today.

Janice Mirikitani, Sansei poet laureate, having been interned in Arkansas as a child, became a revolutionary artist and proponent of social justice, and brought her own passion to co-creating the Glide Foundation. Janice embodied compassion amidst grit in the Tenderloin. She was a force who helped define social justice in S.F., committed to giving voice to the most marginalized, giving access to food, housing, recovery tools, and opportunities to grow. Together, she and Cecil changed the face of inclusion in San Francisco. Their legacy continues through the many programs and advocacy they offered.
https://www.glide.org/

I Think in Pictures

Mother meant well,
believed in her,
and advocated for her progress.
but no one understood
the magic back then
with institutionalization recommended.
That summer on her aunt's farm
opened the first of many doors,
a concept introduced
by a favorite science teacher,
with her first cowboy connection
affirming animal truths.
Perspective of a blind roommate
offered still more new visions.
The distinction between moos
at first ridiculed
but finally proofed
giving them their due respect,
while knowing that the world
needs all kinds of minds.

May we all aspire for our lives
to have such meaning.

Temple Grandin—her story

'There are the math and science geniuses at the heart of life-altering accomplishments, but the geeks and the misfits and the kids with labels are the ones who actually build the stuff.'

Diagnosed with Autism at age four, with institutionalization the norm, Temple was encouraged to explore everything, something that she advocates today in her international talks on behalf of those with Autism. Her introduction to her aunt's farm, the summer before college, was in having to get out of the car to open the gate. She immediately saw the angles and the process in her mind and shortly developed a system to open the gate automatically. She saw things in pictures. Despite the broad lack of understanding of Autism in her youth, she persevered in pursuing inventions, systems and advocacy. Attending a conference with her mother in 1981, she spoke up to clarify what her experience was and what did, in fact work for calming. Now in her seventies, incredibly poised, while no less passionate about her beliefs, and a professor at Colorado State University with a doctorate, her determination drives her teaching about the preciousness of life and the vital need for a return to hands-on classes for all children. She lectures worldwide. Meanwhile, she has revolutionized the cattle processing industry and made huge strides in the equine therapy realm. Different, but definitely not less.

Assertive and Aggressive

Always immersed in numbers
high school graduate at fourteen
Doctorate at eighteen

Choosing an unlikely path
as a research mathematician
Even before awareness of
such a thing as orbital mechanics
or Azimuth angles

Her boundless curiosity vaulting her
through glass ceilings
trailblazing for so many

First a part of the pool of
computers in skirts.
First to have her name on a report at NASA
Calculating gust elevation
and Shepard's moon trajectory

Dismissing segregation and misogyny
Trusted by John Glenn
to calculate celestial bodies

Finally awarded the medal of freedom by Obama
On BBC's list of 100 Women of influence worldwide
Her accuracy drove confidence in new technology

Katherine Johnson—her story

At a family gathering in 1952, a relative mentioned that the National Advisory Committee for Aeronautics (NACA) was hiring mathematicians, thus setting her career course.

Johnson's work included calculating trajectories, launch windows, and emergency return paths for Project Mercury spaceflights, including those for astronauts Alan Shepard, the first American in space, and John Glenn, the first American in orbit, and rendezvous paths for the Apollo Lunar Module and command module on flights to the Moon. Katherine (and a colleague) were temporarily assigned to help the all-male flight research team. Katherine›s knowledge of analytic geometry helped make quick allies of male bosses and colleagues to the extent that, "they forgot to return me to the pool." While the racial and gender barriers were always there, Katherine ignored them. Katherine was assertive, asking to be included in editorial meetings as the first woman. She simply told people she had done the work and that she belonged.

When NASA used electronic computers for the first time to calculate John Glenn's orbit around Earth, officials called on Johnson to verify the computer's numbers; Glenn had asked for her specifically and had refused to fly unless Johnson verified the calculations, marking the turning point in the U.S./Soviet space race.

She was presented with the Silver Snoopy Award by NASA astronaut Leland D. Melvin and a NASA Group Achievement Award. She was a lead character in the 2016 film *Hidden Figures*. In 2019, Johnson was awarded the Congressional Gold Medal by the United States Congress. In 2021, she was inducted posthumously into the National Women's Hall of Fame.

Unnamed Warriors

Some remain unknown, unnamed, uncounted.
Perhaps a certain amount of culture, tradition in play.
Imagine someone faceless, anonymous,
saving your life . . .
Asking that we explore our own responses
had it been our choice, perhaps our duty.
Elders stepped up, unconcerned with
reproductive damage.
Cancers did occur.

Nature advancing beyond imagination
on both land and sea.
Easy, now, to speak of maintenance
and possibilities,
as the repercussions remain vague
and the quarantine remains.

Synonymous with disaster over a decade later,
decommissioning efforts continue.
The numbers wavered and grew,
but they were always reverently referenced
as the Fukushima Fifty.

The Fukushima Fifty—their story

In March of 2011, the 9.0 Tōhoku earthquake in Japan was followed by a tsunami of unimagined forty-six-foot height, rupturing and flooding the Daiichi nuclear power plant. There were three explosions in multiple reactors, melting fuel rods within, flooding the back-up generators and leaking radiation into the air and ocean. All power was lost, including the cooling systems essential to cooling the reactors. Over 150,000 people were evacuated from the area, some never to return and the quarantine around the perimeter of the plant remains today. The disaster relief workers continued on site, despite aftershocks and rising levels of radiation. Older workers offered to replace younger, citing long-term health effects and reproductive impact. Millions of lives were spared by the courageous technicians who remained for damage control.

Their unflinching bravery and selflessness provided a legacy attesting to the human spirit when faced with crisis.

Choices

(Reflections on the film, *The Hail Mary Project*)

Would you opt to be the hero?
Alone in your demise.
Or rather to remain with all others
in shared agony and angst.
Connection paramount.

And then if there were no choice . . .
how would you show up?

While making peace
with your role in humanity,
a new lesson is presented.
Another chance
to share the journey.
To learn how precious
one being can be.
Connection.
The value of shared intention.
Accompanying dilemmas.
To save yourself
or another.
Your world or theirs.
Unity.   Shared goals.
Potential for shared triumph.
Validating new values.
Possibilities unimagined.

Life's cycles
and circles
returning to our
true selves
with accompanying gifts

and always with more choices.

Gratitudes

Remembering to pause for gratitude is such a vital piece of the work these days, a practice in shifting how we move through this journey.

Stewart Warren gets a lot of the credit for jump-starting this project about eight years ago. He was always the best at making me believe in myself and in making me feel seen.

A big dose of gratitude to the Silver City Poetic Outlaws for listening to random hero poems, whether fitting for the moment or not. Blessings, Shelly Barnett and Christophe Maso for giving us a safe space to grow and thrive. And to the Tranquilbuzz coffee house and heart of our community, for their generous open mics.

Thanks, too, to my beta readers, Pamela Morgan, Lynne Zotalis, and Hank Blackwell, and to all of those who kept asking how it was going throughout all the intervening years. You fueled my momentum.

My deep appreciation to all my online resources like the 'Jon S. Randal Peace Page, ' 'Chronicles Through Lenses,' and 'Amazing Stories' for supplying such good fodder and for continuing to keep me positive, despite all the reasons not to be, in this uncertain time.

It was definitely self-serving to encourage Arnell Ando to move to Silver City where I have better access to her Photoshop skills and generous heart. And my thanks to Leslie Katz-Josepher and Belynda Webb for offering a photographer's eye to the cover creation.

I am reminded what a leap of faith it is to request cover blurbs in this time of faulty technology. (Did they get the email or did it go to spam? Did they just not want to be put on the spot for something positive? Did they forget who I was, despite my deep respect for them?) Sigh. It makes me still more awed by the abundance of those who stepped up and offered such glowing terms to inspire your reading of this book. You are all my heroes.

E PLURIBUS UNUM
AXLE
CONTEMPORARY

About the Author

Pamela Warren Williams is a poet and artist, with a fine art and design background, and a lifelong habit of artistic expression. Her heartland upbringing provided the springboard for thirty expansive years in the San Francisco area, where the vibrant culture, spectacular geography, and her antique/collectible business offered a parade of provocative fodder for her voice. New Mexico's extreme contrasts and rich history are now fueling alchemical inspiration and empowerment through its proffered seductions and mysterious remnants of multi-cultural heritage, feeding her current writing work and her rebirthing of her late husband's publishing business. She searches out poignant truths provoked by the heartbreaking beauty of a miniature wing on her studio floor, or the current pain on our border and in so much of this country and follows the ties that either bind or tear us apart. Her poems and assemblages have appeared in the *Poets Speak: Walls and Survival* anthologies, four *Lummox* anthologies, *Live Out Loud, We Don't Break* anthology, *Poetry Lovers* and *Writing in a Woman's Voice* epubs, *ElPalacio.org,* and her own collections, *Hair On Fire* and *You Always Near, The Stewart Poems* (Mercury HeartLink) as well as the *Upward Spiral* anthology, with Shelly Barnett, Leonore Hildebrandt, and Lynne Zotalis. Her writing is most recently driven by stories of heroic actions, both current and historical, celebrating our connections and inspiring diving more deeply into the miracles and grace of this journey.

www.ingramcontent.com/pod-product-compliance
Lightning Source LLC
LaVergne TN
LVHW080311110826
845155LV00023B/113

* 9 7 8 1 9 4 9 6 5 2 4 8 2 *